MEDITATION FOR ADULTS MASTERY

The Ultimate Storybook To Avoid Anxiety, Fear, Panic And Insomnia With Calm And Warm Stories For Adults

WALT PIXAR

© **Copyright 2021 - All rights reserved.**

The content contained within this book may not be reproduced, duplicated or transmitted without direct written permission from the author or the publisher.

Under no circumstances will any blame or legal responsibility be held against the publisher, or author, for any damages, reparation, or monetary loss due to the information contained within this book. Either directly or indirectly.

Legal Notice:

This book is copyright protected. This book is only for personal use. You cannot amend, distribute, sell, use, quote or paraphrase any part, or the content within this book, without the consent of the author or publisher.

Disclaimer Notice:

Please note the information contained within this document is for educational and entertainment purposes only. All effort has been executed to present accurate, up to date, and reliable, complete information. No warranties of any kind are declared or implied. Readers acknowledge that the author is not engaging in the rendering of legal, financial, medical or professional advice. The content within this book has been derived from various sources. Please consult a licensed professional before attempting any techniques outlined in this book.

By reading this document, the reader agrees that under no circumstances is the author responsible for any losses, direct or indirect, which are incurred as a result of the use of information contained within this document, including, but not limited to, errors, omissions, or inaccuracies.

Table of Contents

INTRODUCTION

This book is here to emphasize just how important your own life choices are when it comes to the stress that you endure. The way that you live is important. The way that you choose to handle your stress matters immensely and you need to be able to figure out how you wish to cope.

Do you want to be the person that is a ball of tension constantly, snapping at people and worrying about every little action that you take, or do you want to be that person that is able to better understand yourself and those around you thanks to the ways in which you respond to the world at large? Do you want to master your stress once and for all or do you want to figure out how else you can manage it?

When you want to work, you need to keep in mind one thing: Your choices that you make and the lifestyle that you choose to live, whether that is one of positivity or negativity, or that is one of being afraid or letting your anxieties run rampant, is going to determine everything.

Your life is made up of the choices you make, and while you cannot control the world, you can control the ways in which you respond to the world, and sometimes, that makes all the difference in the world.

CHAPTER 1: SLEEP IS THE MIRROR OF YOUR DAY

Imagine for a moment that you have just woken up for the day. Your mind and body feel heavy and slow. Every part of your body aches in protest as you force yourself to get up, your eyes struggling to stay open. Then, you spend your day, grumpy, sluggish, and yearning to get right back into your bed. You desperately want to return to bed, and your attitude shows it. You find that you are snappier than ever; you do not want to tolerate the way that people talk to you. You do not have the patience to get through your day. You drink a coffee as you run out the door for work, another at lunch, and yet another as you head home. You are not present with your children; when you are home with them during the evening, you find that you do not want to work with them. You do not want to play, not because you don't care, but because you are too tired. You rush through bedtime routine, snapping at your children and your partner, and then you rush through cleaning up after dinner, and by the time that you finally collapse into bed, you realize that you only have 5 hours to sleep before you get up and do it all again.

Now, imagine that you wake up one morning *before* your alarm clock. You're wide-eyed and happy. You're ready to face the day. You're ready to head out to work and your alarm hasn't even gone off yet! You stretch in bed, slowly, calmly, and feel like your body is ready to take on anything. You get up, skip the coffee, have time to take your time getting ready to go to work. You make a nutritious breakfast for you and your family, and off you go. You spend your entire day in a good mod; you're relaxed and happy, and more importantly, you feel like you can think clearly. You feel like you can think clearly and effectively. You feel like you can tackle anything that you need to get done, all because your mind is clear. You get to have a nice evening with your children, spending time with them after they get home from school, they get off to bed, and you finish up with everything that you needed to do. Since you were well-rested to begin with, you find that you are much quicker and much more efficient than you normally were when sleep-deprived, and you get to bed right on time.

Sleep is essential. It takes up hours of your day, and just because you are laying on the bed and not actively engaged in anything does not mean that you are wasting time. It is critical to ensuring that you are well rested. It is essential to making sure that your mind is sharp and your body is well-rested. It is necessary to help you feel like you are ready to tackle your day. It is imperative that you do not skip out on your sleep; you need it to ensure that your body can function, and it is also good for your mind as well. Sleep heals the body. It helps memory. It manages the immune system. It is a normal, basic need.

More importantly, it is the mirror of your day. The sleep that you get will reflect the ay that you will have. If you want to have a good day, you need to also have a good night the night prior. It will set the stage for everything that you need; if you sleep well, you encourage good mental wellbeing. If you want to make sure that you start your day on the best possible foot, you will be best served by making sure that your sleep is right.

Think about it; when you wake up after a bad night, you are tired. You are grumpy. You are miserable thanks to the fact that your nighttime sleep sets you up for the day. As your nighttime sleep gets better, your daytime energy levels are more stable.

Along those same lines, your waking hours and the way that you spend them directly impact the sleep that you get later on as well. If you spend your day constantly stressing out about the world around you, you are going to see other problems. You are going to feel like you are stressed out and tense. You are going to feel like you struggle when you try to sleep; you may suffer from insomnia. You may find that the sleep that you do get is poor, or you wake up a lot, rolling back and forth and desperately trying to get to sleep.

However, the fact that your night and day are mirrored is a good thing; it means that, since they are endlessly intertwined with each other, you are able to impact both of them at the exact same time. You are able to make sure that you are able to fix your sleep by fixing your daytime, and vice versa, in repairing your sleep, you also fix the energy levels and the attitudes that you have in the day. They endlessly feed into each other, creating compelling reasons for you to work hard and make sure that, day and night, you are attempting to be the healthiest that you can be.

CHAPTER 2: THE SCIENCE OF SLEEP: HOW TO PROMOTE GOOD HEALTH

We spend roughly 8 hours out of each 24 sleeping—that is 1/3 of our time. This time is spent, laying, motionless in bed without doing anything at all. It is spent not working, not acting, or doing anything else. If you were to look at someone that was sleeping, you would see someone motionless; you would assume that they are being lazy, or that they are wasting their time. They are clearly not doing anything productive with their time, right?

That's actually entirely wrong; sleep is actually incredibly active, even if you cannot view the activity by looking at them. You cannot see the activity that is happening, but that does not mean that nothing is happening at all. In fact, within the brain, and even on a cellular level, sleep is incredibly powerful. We do not yet know why we have evolved to go through sleep, however, it is something that has been documented in the vast majority of the animal kingdom.

Scientists have endlessly researched sleep, looking for why it occurs, how it matters and the ways in which different animals sleep. Some sleep nearly endlessly and others sleep for the vast majority of their time alive. Some species of bats, for example, will sleep for upwards of 20 hours a day. Others appear to not sleep very long at all; giraffes only sleep for around 30 minutes within that 24 hour period. Humans seem to fall somewhere in the middle; they sleep for around 8 hours a day, and they need that or they begin to suffer from the effects of sleep deprivation.

Restful Sleep and Good Health

Restful sleep is essential if you want to maintain a healthy lifestyle; a good night's sleep becomes imperative to ensuring proper wellbeing, and it does so by resting the body. There are some very important, and even compelling reasons that you should always work hard to ensure that your own sleep is restful. These tendencies toward restful sleep can help your body and mind. You may never have realized it, but those benefits that you can have are incredibly compelling.

Sleep helps your body to relax. It happens by releasing tensions and allowing the body to heal. There are many anti-inflammatory events that happen when you are sleeping and they primarily occur thanks to the fact that, at the end of the day, sleep is a time for healing. You do not just miss out on those anti-inflammatory effects when you are not getting the sleep that you need, however; you also experience higher levels of stress. You experience stress levels that are elevated when you do not sleep enough; that means that you are literally making your body suffer the effects of stress more than ever before if you do not get enough sleep.

Restful sleep limits the amount of stress that your body is exposed to. It keeps the stress levels lower to allow for other parts of your body to thrive. This is thanks to the effect that stress has on the entire body, which we will be getting to shortly; rather, when you stress, your body is exposed to a state of natural relaxation. You encourage your body to rest and allow for parts of it to work less. Your heart, for example, does not need to beat so quickly when you are resting. Your heart is able to slow down, as does your breathing, because when you are lying down on your bed and sleeping, you are not going to be actively moving around. Your head is on level with your heart, so you do not have to worry about pumping blood up higher into your brain. This allows for a natural decline in blood pressure as well. Because of this, sleeping well and getting restful sleep in general is also associated very closely with being able to lower your blood pressure.

Even that is not the end of the numerous benefits that your body gains by sleeping well and regularly. Your body is also able to boost its immune response. It is able to create all of the necessary proteins and cells that your body uses in order to fend off infections, making it imperative to remaining healthy. Sleep and getting ample rest is perhaps one of the best ways that you are able to boost your immune system and keep you from getting sick.

Sleep will also help you maintain your weight. It may not necessarily help you lose weight, but when you sleep regularly, you do regulate out the hormones in your body. You are able to regulate out the appetite, and by making sure that the appetite *is* regulated out properly, you also allow your body to reduce those cravings that may otherwise bust the diet.

Sleep is something that you need, not just because you are tired, but because during your sleep, you regulate out so many very important functions and without it, you would struggle. You will struggle to stay awake. You will struggle to stay healthy. You will struggle to work and keep your mind clear. You will struggle to regulate your mood and your energy levels. At the end of the day, remaining consistent in your sleep is perhaps one of the best things that you can do for yourself to help ensure that, at the end of the day, you are happy and healthy.

Sleep, Sleep Cycles, and You

We sleep frequently. So frequently, in fact, that it is a daily occurrence for the vast majority of us! However, despite the fact that, during sleep, you are simply laying in your bed, there is much more going on. There are changes to the way that your body and your brain are active during sleep. These changes happen in a very predictable cycle and they occur for reasons that are believed to be biological. They are related to the biological internal clocks that we have, and extensive study has revealed that we all go through these cycles in five distinct stages that typically occur in a very specific order.

Understanding the order of the stages of sleep becomes essential to remember; you need to keep in mind how long these are so you can ensure that you wake up at the right time. When you can keep sleep cycles in mind, you can make sure that you wake up at precisely the right time at any point in time. You will do this to make sure that, ultimately, you are as well-rested as you can be. Think about it—have you ever been woken up at a point where you were uncomfortable? Perhaps you woke up feeling foggy. This is referred to as sleep inertia and it usually happens when you wake up suddenly and unexpectedly during REM sleep. Your body was not ready to wake up naturally, so it struggled. This is because your body is still full of melatonin; it is still full of the hormones that are responsible for feeling sleepy, so you wake up feeling uncomfortable, groggy, and you may even just fall back asleep. If there were ever a recipe for the wrong kind of sleep that you can get, it is the kind in which you are woken up in the middle of a cycle.

Because there are very clear points in time where you can be woken up that are better than others, it becomes important that you work as hard as you can to ensure that you are always waking up at the right time. Ensuring that you keep that in mind means that you are able to wake up at exactly the right time.

The first stage of sleep is the light stage—this is perhaps the shortest stage of them all. During this stage, you go through a period of just a few minutes, typically between five and ten, in which your body and mind begin to slow down. You begin to feel relaxed and start to doze off. This is the period of sleep in which you are not deeply asleep at all. It is very easy to wake up during this stage, and sometimes, you may not even realize that you have fallen asleep in the first place. Any power napping, if you try to use them, should be less than 20 minutes to make sure that you wake up during this stage. Any longer than that 15 or 20 minutes will require you to sleep for at least an entire cycle, or you are likely to feel worse than before napping.

In stage two, you are still in a lighter sleep. However, your body begins to relax even further. Your brain is beginning to slow down and your mind is preparing to sleep deeply. This stage is marked by a lessening in muscle and brain activity, though there are, on an EEG chart, notable spikes in brain activity. These are believed to be important for memory consolidation, which is a process that is largely based in sleep. This is what allows for memories that are in your short term storage to be moved to long term to allow for recall later on. While scientist do not yet have a way to definitively discover this yet, they do believe that the vast majority of your long-term memories occur during sleep.

As stage two comes to an end, you enter what is known as deep sleep. This is most notable because of the lessened brain activity that can be seen on EEGs. During these stages of sleep, you are usually much harder to wake. Your sleep becomes deeper and your entire body begins to relax. Stages three and four are both slow wave sleep, and typically the body is entirely limp. This stage is also very important for the body. In this stage, however, you are working hard on the body. Your body is preparing itself to grow, if applicable, through the production of growth hormones. It involves activating the immune system and ensuring that it can work to help fix any wear and tear on the body. The body is full of all sorts of wear and tear—it is very important for the body to be able to go through these stages to ensure that your body is healthy and that your body can recover as necessary. Your body spends most of its time in these stages.

As stage four comes to a close, however, the body begins to enter the dreaming state. During dreams, many different areas of the body can be found to be active, much like how they are during waking time. However, unlike during waking time, the body is paralyzed. During this period of time, your body is able to paralyze itself so you do not act out the dreams that you are in. Think about it—when you dream, you are experiencing these events around you. You may feel like they are very real and because of that, and because the brain acts in ways that are similar to the dreams being real in the first place, it would be very possible for the body to simply respond to everything as if it were awake. That could be a major cause for concern; you could, for example, find that you hit someone else when you were trying to get by in your dream. You could walk out, hurt yourself, or otherwise do something problematic, all because you are unconsciously acting out whatever is happening during your dreams.

As you dream, your body is in stage five; this is where you go through the rapid eye movement associated with the REM stage. During this stage, your body is going to be much more active. You will experience fluctuations of heart rate and blood pressure, quite possibly thanks to the dreams that you are having. Your breathing will shift during this stage as well. We do not yet know exactly what goes on during REM sleep, but neuroscientists are pretty sure that it is responsible for both learning and memory, thanks to the way that the brain is able to process and consolidate.

Good Sleep vs. Bad Sleep

When it comes to the sleep that you get, it is much more important to focus on the quality. It is essential that, during your sleeping hours, your sleep is as high-quality as possible to ensure that you get the full benefit from it. However, it is still important to get the right amount of sleep as well. If you cannot align your sleep quantity and quality, you can begin to suffer from other problems as well. You may find that, sometimes, getting 10 hours of poor sleep is not actually better than getting 6 hours of good, restful sleep.

While it may be the case that people are better off with less sleep that is restful than more poor sleep, you should consider the fact that, at the end of the day, as a human being, you still have some recommendations in terms of how long you sleep in the first place. In particular, it is important for you to sleep somewhere between seven and nine hours a night, if you are trying to perfectly optimize the sleep that you get, but at the end of the day, it is even more important for you to make sure that the sleep that you do get is quality. Keep in mind that for some people, they may do well with just 6 hours of sleep on a regular basis while other people actually need more sleep. This is not because they are lazier; their bodies simply have different requirements that need to be considered as well. To discover the right amount of sleep for you, you will need to do some trial and error. You may find that eight hours is perfect for you, or you may already be feeling groggy or jetlagged after seven. You need to work to discover what works precisely for you, and then you should stick to it.

In terms of quality, then, you must aim for the best that you can give yourself. This means that, most of the time, you are working to provide yourself with sleep that is good. Good sleep is defined quite simply; it involves falling asleep quickly when you get in bed for the night. It involves sound sleep throughout the night that is defined as either sleeping through the night or only waking up once and then going back to sleep relatively quickly as well.

By quickly, here, it is important to note that 30 minutes is the cutoff. You should be able to fall asleep within 30 minutes of getting in bed, according to the experts, and if you can do that, as well as ensure that you are able to stay sleep, or fall asleep within 20 minutes of waking up another time, your sleep is defined as good. This means that there is a pretty liberal amount of time there for you to fall asleep healthily. There are no rules, by any means, in which falling asleep has to be instant, and for most people, unless they are exhausted already, they are not going to. Going to sleep takes time thanks to all of the processes that have to occur and thanks to everything that your mind has to do to prepare for it.

Bad quality sleep, then, is anything else. If you regularly find yourself tossing in turning in bed, or staring at the ceiling in exasperation, you are showing signs of bad sleep quality. Sleep should not be a struggle. It should not be something that you dread. It should be something that you welcome and invite into your life; a part of your daily routine that you look forward to, and if you do not, then there may be a disconnect somewhere. Perhaps you have a problem with quality or quantity. Perhaps you have some outside factors that are weighing in on you. No matter what the reason, however, if you struggle to sleep now, there are ways that you can fix the problem.

If you already suffer from poor sleep, there is good news for you; most people are able to get out of that rut of poor sleep quality relatively simply. If quantity is the problem, all you have to do is figure out how best to rearrange your schedule. There are almost always different ways in which you are able to change up your daily schedule in order to guarantee that the time that you need for sleep is present; you simply have to learn to take it and to make sleep a priority in your life the same way that you must prioritize getting the healthy food that you need and the exercise to keep your body healthy.

If quality is the problem, there are other fixes that you can implement as well. They will be more involved, but with the optimal lifestyle changes, you can oftentimes find that you can completely remedy the problem. It may not be easy, and you may feel like it is an impossible feat sometimes, but it is an important one to remember. Certain actions and lifestyle changes, such as making sure that you exercise more, or limiting the consumption of evening caffeine, or even alcohol, can actually greatly relieve the problems. There are mindset changes that you can make as well to help ensure that the sleep that you get is restful. If you are the kind of person that tosses and turns in bed, reliving each and every embarrassment that you have ever suffered through, you may find that it is difficult to fall asleep, but there are ways of slowing those intrusive, obsessive thoughts. There are ways of shifting your thinking away from that negativity and anxiety to allow you to achieve that degree of relaxation that you will need to ensure that you actually can, in fact, rest. This does not have to be difficult, either; you simply need to invest the time to change your mindset, which will be done within this book as well.

CHAPTER 3: DELETING DAILY STRESS: PREPARING FOR RELAXATION

Perhaps one of the biggest threats to good, quality sleep, aside from sheer lack of time itself, is stress. Stress can very easily leave you rolling around in bed, struggling to fall asleep and then suffering the consequences the very next day. However, there is a slight problem with this—when you do not get the sleep that you need because you are stressed in the first place, you actually just make the problem worse. The less that you sleep and the more tired that you feel, the more likely it is that, at the end of the day, you feel even more stressed out than before. If you feel stressed out, you will get even less sleep than the night before and it will endlessly perpetuate into this loop of insomnia.

Now, insomnia will be the great point of discussion in the next chapter, but for now, you must remember a very important point: Stress in excess is bad for you. While stress has a very normal purpose and has a very normal way that it can be used in ways that are actually evolutionarily beneficial to the survival of the species, it can also be very harmful in many ways. It can negatively impact the body and it can negatively impact the mind. You need to understand these negative implications so you can then begin to fix the problem, as it is only when you begin to fix the problem that you can actually get out of that stress rut.

Now, stress can have many different causes, many of which are also legitimate. It is legitimate and valid to be stressed out, for example, if you cannot make ends meet financially. It is valid to be stressed or worried if someone that you love or care for deeply is currently ill. It is certainly valid to feel stressed when you are dealing with other problems that are negatively impacting your life. However, there are also things that you can do about it. You can learn, for example, how you can defeat that stress. You can learn to stop it from taking control of you and you can learn to alleviate it. This does not necessarily mean that you will be fixing the cause of the stressor that you are suffering from; in many instances, you are simply changing up the way in which you respond to them in the first place. After all, it is very important to remember that you must be willing to accept what you cannot control, but to control what you can.

Stress and Your Body

Stress is a very normal response to anything that is considered a change. You can even have very positive events, such as getting a new job or having a child, become marred by stress. This is not because they are negative, per se, but rather, they require you to change. They require you to adjust to respond to them in some way, and it may be in a way that you were not prepared to accept, or in a way that you do not want to accept. Stress is very normal, and it happens in response to the world around you.

Now, you may be thinking, if stress is something automatic in response to the environment, which you cannot always control, and in fact, most of the time, you may not be able to control it at all, then would you always be enslaved to that stress? Is it impossible to break free from that commotion and discomfort? Is it impossible to truly live a stress-free life when that stress can control you?

To be fair, you cannot control the environment. You cannot make sure that the people around you only work in the ways that you ask them to. You cannot ensure that you do not suddenly get into a car accident on your way to work, and you cannot ensure that your children will cooperate with you when you need them to go to sleep at night. You cannot control what your friends and family will do or how they will treat you. In fact, there is very little in this great, big, vast world that you actually *can* truly control. Nevertheless, there is one very important factor that you can: Your reaction.

Before we fully address what it means to be stressed, it is important to note the purpose of stress in the first place. It is your body's natural response when something seems abnormal. It is there so your body can stop and begin to cope with it; it is there so your body can prepare itself to respond to whatever the stressor it. The stress starts by your body trying to identify what the cause for alarm is, and that can very quickly develop into fear or anxiety, or it can lead to anger as well.

In the short-term, feelings of stress can be good. They can give you that needed push that you need to push through to achieve that deadline on your work that you have to do. They can make you focus on the world around you, becoming more alert so you can figure out whether or not something that is happening is dangerous or a threat to you. This enables you to have that added energy, or adrenaline, to figure out if what is happening around you is something that will be harmful to you. Think of the feeling of tenseness that you feel when you see someone approaching you unexpectedly; you may immediately tense up as your body and mind quickly figure out whether or not this person is a threat to you. This is normal, and without this kind of stress, we as a species would likely take far fewer precautions than we should be. We would likely get ourselves into far more dangerous situations than we should, simply because we do not feel that pressure from the stress to keep us on track.

Long-term, however, stress becomes a problem. Also known as chronic stress, when your body is constantly operating in this sort of capacity, you will begin to see some serious detriments. They may not even be noticeable to you at first, and they may be minor, especially in the earlier days. However, there are some very important warning signs that you should always consider when it comes to the stress that your body is enduring. Keep in mind that, when you are under chronic stress, however, your body is suffering. The signs of chronic stress can seriously hurt your body in ways that you may not even consider. Some of the most common warning signs that your body is under too much stress, however, include:

- Feeling dizzy or distant
- Suffering from unexplained pain, aches, or general malaise
- Tensing your jaw, sometimes even grinding teeth
- Suffering from headaches
- Insomnia and struggling to sleep
- Changes from your normal appetite, either seeing it increase or decrease
- Suffering from indigestion or other digestive tract issues
- Exhaustion, paired with insomnia
- Shakiness or trembling
- Tension throughout the body

- Feeling like your heart is racing

When you suffer from stress, however, there is so much more going on in your body. During stress, your body is enduring what is known as the "fight or flight" response. During this, it feels like it is in some sort of danger, either physical or otherwise, but the body does not discriminate between the effects of physical danger, such as being threatened by a bear or a dog, or emotional stress, such as worrying about money, having relationship issues, or anything else. The body does not differentiate between the two at all. This means that, just because you are not in any danger at all at that moment does not mean that you will not react with the same visceral emotions and feelings as if you are currently facing financial ruin, or on the verge of divorce. It is all the same to your body, and you will still see the same hormones coursing through your veins.

In particular, during stress, your body is full of two hormones that are primarily responsible for the response to it: Adrenaline and cortisol. They are both very powerful hormones that can leave you reeling; you can feel like your heart is pounding. This is because, when you are under genuine, life-threatening peril, your body is trying to survive, and ultimately, the best way to survive is through ensuring that the body can properly react. This means that the body must have enough oxygen throughout it to enable it to move accordingly. Your breathing will be quicker, too, allowing you to bring in more oxygen quicker than ever.

Under this stress as well, your body prioritizes diverting blood away from the digestive tract and instead, it expends that energy elsewhere. This means that digestion begins to slow down, but at the same time, the stress also pushes your liver to release glucose into the body as well. Glucose is blood sugar that is oftentimes stored in order to be used at a later time, if necessary. It is there to give your body energy when it needs it the most, and when you are stressed, your body thinks that you need the energy to escape from that bear or that lion that wants to eat you, when in reality, you may be sitting at a table, surrounded by bills, or having a heated argument with someone. Nevertheless, the longer you are under this stress, the more glucose is pumped throughout the body. The more glucose that you have pumped within your body, the more likely that it becomes that your body is not able to keep up with it. After long enough of keeping all of that excessive glucose in your blood, you become at an increased risk of developing type 2 diabetes.

During this stress, you are also likely to feel your entire body tense up. Tension happens as your body's way to try to protect itself; it tenses up in hopes of avoiding becoming damaged. However, if you do not pay close enough attention, it is entirely possible that you actually end up holding onto that tension, and it can build up in your entire body. When that happens, after long enough, you begin to ache. Your tight muscles can begin to hurt your body, and after a while, they can begin to hurt your head, too. You can even begin clenching your jaws and running the risk of actually grinding your teeth, too.

The constant state of stress also leads to inflammation; during the time that you are stressed out, your immune system is not able to work as effectively as it normally does, and because it cannot work effectively, those that suffer from stress are also typically more susceptible to being sick as well. They can find that they take longer to heal when they get hurt, and it takes them longer to recover when they do get sick.

Finally, stress can also impact both sexuality and the reproductive cycle as well. When you are constantly stressed out, you can see a direct effect on both men and women. Men may get a boost in testosterone at first, but over time, the levels begin to drop, and this can lead to problems with sperm production. For women, as they become more and more stressed out, they can impact their menstrual cycle. Intense stress can lead to it becoming irregular. Both of these can lead to direct impacts on general fertility of the individuals. Beyond just that, libido typically takes a nosedive during periods of stress, and for good reason; when you are in your fight or flight response, your body is in the exact opposite response from the one of relaxation, which sometimes goes by names such as, "rest and digest," or "feed and breed."

Stress and Your Sleep

Unfortunately, when you are stuck in this loop of stress, you do find that it is difficult to sleep. This is intentional by design; can you imagine just how difficult it would be if you were trying your hardest to keep yourself or your family alive, but you were completely overcome by exhaustion and sleepiness? Think about it—your emotions and your feelings, including those of stress, were developed by nature. They were nature's way of trying to facilitate the ability of the living beings to stay alive. It involved ample time being redirected toward what mattered most, and usually, what mattered the most was survival. That meant that animals needed to be alert. They needed to be highly responsive to the world around them. They needed to be able to feel like they could respond at a moment's notice to anything that they were threatened with and that could only really happen if they were able to, more or less, turn off the sleepiness.

Unfortunately, when your stress becomes chronic, as it often does in this world full of endless unnatural responsibilities, such as bills that need to get paid or the work project that needs to get done, this can take its toll. You can begin to see these same degrees of stress play out over and over again. You can struggle to fall asleep when you need it the most and you can toss and turn all night long. Because your body is full or that adrenaline and cortisol, you are not going to feel tired. Or rather, you may feel completely exhausted, but if your body is so full of those stress hormones that are compelling it to act, tense up, and be alert, you are not going to be able to sleep. That might be great for that one-time deadline, but if it happens on the regular, you are going to really struggle to get everything done the way it needs to be. When that happens, what you need to do is learn how to turn the stress off.

Relaxing Your Body
Oftentimes, some of the best ways that you can defeat that stress is through making use of relaxation methods. These are some of the first lines of offense that are taken when you

find that you are struggling to sleep. If you are struggling to sleep, you will oftentimes be given methods that you can try to use to help your body fall asleep. Sometimes, you will find that the way that your body is going to be served best is through exercising beforehand. There are several different ways that you can begin to aid your body in relaxing. Ultimately, the ways in which you are able to begin relaxing your body can be thought of in two ways: They can be bottom-up and top-down.

Bottom-up methods of relaxation focus on changing your body in order to influence your mind. Essentially, you will do something to your body, whether that is breathing, muscle relaxation, or any other method that involves you focusing on making changes to the way you use your body. When you make use of these sorts of relaxation methods, you are trying to convince your mind to take note that, thanks to the way that your body is moving or the way that your body is behaving, there is not threat or stress. One example is the use of salivation—when you are stressed out, your body releases the cortisol and adrenaline that we have been talking about. When it does that, you will naturally begin to salivate less. This is because salivating is not essential to keeping yourself safe, so it gets deemed unnecessary to maintain when precious resources are being diverted elsewhere instead. When you make yourself salivate, then, such as through eating something tasty, or even visualizing something that you love to eat, your mind catches on. It realizes that, since you are salivating, it cannot possibly be stressed, as it never salivates when there is real danger present.

Top-down methods of relaxation are the exact opposite— they focus on changing your way of thinking so you can then begin to slow down the stress in your body. These are ways that you are able to talk your stress out, for example. Or, you may find that these are methods such as using mindfulness, or such as trying to meditate. Meditation and mindfulness both have a direct impact on the body, but they are both primarily states of mind. When you use them, you change the mind and the mindset, which then leads to changing the body as well to ensure that it also begins to relax. There are many different ways in which you are able to encourage and facilitate the relaxation through top-down methods.

Ultimately, as you continue to read through this book, you will be introduced to them all. You will see some methods that are bottom-up, such as Chapter 8 and the focus on yoga techniques to help you begin to move your body. You will be introduced to techniques in Chapter 3 that will guide you through breathing deeply and muscle relaxation to help you begin to slow down the stress that your body is feeling. As you let go of all that tension, you will find that sleeping becomes easier than ever. Throughout most of this book, however, the focus will be on top-down relaxation techniques. You will be focusing on how you can change the thinking that you have. You will be taking a look at how you can change your mindset and your own mental habits that can help in ensuring that, at the end of the day, you can better cope with the stressors that you are under. You will take look at how to meditate, how to be mindful, and how to visualize.

Overall, the only way for you to relax is through ensuring that you understand that the stressors that you have are there. You need to be willing and able to remind yourself of precisely why you may be struggling to sleep in the first place. You need to remember that, at the end of the day, it is okay to be stressed every now and then, and stress is not something itself that is deserving of fear. However, what is deserving of being mitigated is the chronic stressors that people face all too often. You need to be able to defeat that feeling of chronic stress to ensure that, at the end of the day, you can get that good, restful, quality sleep that you deserve.

CHAPTER 4: BASIC BEDTIME STORIES: MINDFULNESS AND VISUALIZATION FOR RELAXATION

Children are not the only ones who benefit from reading bedtime stories. In fact, reading before bed for thirty minutes is calmly recommended in nearly any bedtime routine that is meant to help alleviate insomnia. Bedtime stories work well because they begin to relax you. You have to be mindful when you read if you want to recall the information, and most of the time, the stories that people choose to read before bed are those that are meant to be enjoyed.

When you read, something special happens. You begin to visualize what you are reading. You can hear the characters interacting in your head. You can see the way they interact, and sometimes, you can even begin to see the images provided for you. This is mindful visualization, and as we have already discussed, that can be one way that you can put the brakes on your anxiety or stress and then begin to focus on the moment. You focus on the words on the page in front of you when you read, or on the words being read to you in the case of an audiobook. You are focused. Your body begins to relax.

When you have insomnia, one of the best ways to begin to get your body to relax is through the use of guided meditations and visualization. These stories enable you to, little by little, put together a story and an image in your mind. They allow you to focus on something entirely apart from yourself and allow for you to begin to recognize the images that you are painting in your mind.

The rest of this book will be dedicated to providing you with bedtime stories that are designed to help you relax and unwind. These will be simple guided meditations through imagery to help you calm down. They are stories that are full of images that your mind will enjoy. They are meant to take you to far off scenes and places that perhaps you have dreamed of traveling before, and in visiting them in your mind, focusing on the words of these stories and painting the pictures within your own mind, you will begin to relax.

Remember, as you read through these, that you can make use of meditations like these on your own as well. After reading through all of these stories, you can choose to explore other environments within your own mind as well. You can choose to focus on the world around you, or go visiting places that you never would have imagined. Your mind is one of the most powerful tools that you have and it is one that many people do not take seriously. When you make use of your mind, you are able to visit just about anywhere. There are no hard and fast rules that you must release the idea of imagination just because you are an adult. You do not have to stop imagining grand adventures and wonderful worlds just because you have children of your own. In fact, adventuring within your own imagination is one of the greatest methods that you have available to yourself to allow you to better begin to relax and unwind.

As we move on to the mindfulness and visualization meditations, you want to remember to keep yourself somewhere that is comfortable. These are meditations that are designed to help you fall asleep, so they would be best suited to be read or listened to in the comfort of your own bed when you are entirely ready to sleep. Make sure that you are relaxed. Make sure that you have done everything that you have needed to do beforehand and that you are committed to falling asleep before you start these meditations. They will lose their effectiveness if you are constantly being interrupted or if you stop and start regularly.

The next time that you are ready to use one of these meditations, begin by taking some time to relax beforehand. Take a shower and unwind. Spend some time quieting your mind. Turn off the screens for at least thirty minutes beforehand and stop for a cup of warm tea. Then, when you are finally ready to sleep, get comfortable in bed and begin using these meditations.

CHAPTER 5: THE PRIVATE ISLE

Take a deep breath and close your eyes. Imagine now that you are walking on a sandy beach. The beach has beautiful, white sand, and you can feel it between your bare toes. Each and every step that you take is like a gentle pillow; the sand gently conforms to the shapes of your feet, perfectly balancing your feet and supporting your steps. The sand is incredibly fine and silky as it moves around, and it is warmed by the sun's gentle rays that beam down from the sky. Some of the steps that you take are onto sand that has been gently caressed by the water of the ocean lapping up on shore, and the texture is a little bit different. The sand feels firmer where it is wet, holding its shape more with the water that soaks through it.

A gentle breeze goes by, warm and wet, and tasting faintly of ocean. It glides through your hair and you notice that your shirt gently ripples around you, softly rubbing against your skin. It is a simple, but soft cotton, lightweight and breezy as it tugs around you, and looking down, you realize that it is your favorite color. You have soft shorts on as well, and you are walking, barefoot along the beach. There is no one there with you; for miles and miles around, all you can see is the sand, the water, the sky, and the greenery.

The sun warms your body, first heating up your hair, and then your skin. It is not too hot on this day as you walk along the beach, you notice; in fact, it is the perfect temperature for a relaxing stroll to the cadence of the gentle waves of the water lapping up at the shore. Looking up, you see the cleanest, bluest sky you have ever seen—it is a rich, warm, inviting shade of blue, and there are little wisps of white clouds, barely there, floating above on the gentle wind. They are high up in the sky, just barely breaking up the otherwise even shade of blue everywhere that you can see.

You look to your left and you can see a dense tropical jungle just beyond the sand. Palm fronds shoot up toward the sky from long, spindly tree trunks like a tuft of a lion's tail, leaning over the sand and spreading themselves out as much as they can to soak up the life-giving rays from the sun above.

They are the most verdant green that you have ever seen, and each frond is covered in wide blades that seem to curl upwards, ever-reaching out for the sun. Amidst the base, where all of the fronds come together atop the trunk, you see several round, oblong fruits, nearly the color of a lime. They are coconuts growing above you, and each tree seems to house several of them bunched together. Along the bases of all of the trees, you can see dense growth of bushes that are stretching out, flourishing underneath the sun. They are wide, leafy, and bushy, and you cannot quite tell what they are, but they are even greener, somehow, than the coconut leaves that were dotting the sky above you.

You continue to walk along the quiet beach, step by step. Although you are alone, you do not feel bad at all. You love the quiet solitude as you walk along and the solitude is there to help you as you go along the way. It is quiet, but not too quiet, and you feel at ease, comforted by the waves that you pass by. Soon, you decide to move out from the beach. You move toward the greenery that fills the center of the island. As you go along your way, you see that the bright wall of dense green is really just a wall of bushes that have thrived underneath the sun. Beyond the bushes, you can see that the ground is actually quite walkable, so you continue along.

As you step past the bushes, the air immediately changes. What was once warm and smelling of the sea was suddenly much cooler. The shift from sun to shade was immediately noticeable, but it is still pleasantly comfortable, you are pleased to notice. It is like a whole new world on the other side of the greenery, and as you look around, you realize that you are surrounded by all sorts of wildlife up in the trees. Though they are all carefully out of sight, you can hear that they are all around you. You hear the hundreds of birds singing their songs all around you. Every now and then, you can see the shadow of a bird on the ground beneath you, but every time that you look up, they are gone.

Inside the forest, you notice that there are many fronds and ferns that grow closer to the ground as well. They are a darker green than the green of the plants that are out in the constant sunlight, but they are beautiful in their own ways. You see how some of the fronds, heavy with the blades of the leaves, hang down toward the ground.

The ground underfoot has changed, too. It is soft beneath your feet, but in an earthy, loamy way instead. It no longer sinks underneath your weight, though you can feel that it still has some give. The ground is cool and slightly damp underneath your toes, a sharp contrast from the sand that you had been on just moments prior.

You continue to wander aimlessly throughout the jungle forest. Everywhere that you look, it is more of the same, but constantly changing. There are endless plants and branches, but they are endlessly arranged in different manners. Soon, you see a rock. The rock is the perfect size to sit on, and even is shaped vaguely like a natural seat. You take it, marveling at the smoothness of the stone underneath your hands and let your hand run over its flawless surface. For a rock, it is surprisingly comfortable, and you allow yourself to sit on it and close your eyes, listening to the song of the jungle.

You hear the sounds around you, first as just one endless cacophony around you. It is almost too busy to even comprehend, and it all gets bunched up into one sound: Jungle. But, you can break it up into other sounds, too, if you stop to listen closer. You hear the gentle buzzing of insects all around you, creating the undertone to the entire symphony of sounds that you hear. The gentle undertone of the buzz from the cicadas is punctuated by the occasional chirp of a bird that is nearby. It is high-pitched, but not harsh on the ears; it is a loud chirping that comes in threes each and every time that you hear it pass by. The wind blows through the leaves above you gently, creating a ripple of leaves rubbing against each other. Occasionally, you hear what sounds like a cry of a monkey somewhere in the distance, and some chattering of another animal nearby.

Soon, you can hear different birds, too, all singing together. You can hear the soft trilling song of a bird on the right, high, lilting, and soothing. You can hear a slightly harsher sound to your left, but it is not unpleasant as it sings to you. The songs of the birds all complement each other perfectly. The more you listen, the more layers you seem to uncover in the ever-changing song around you. You can hear the sound of a frog croaking every now and then, punctuating the birds' melodies.

Underneath all of it, however, you hear something else: the unmistakable sound of water babbling over rocks. There must be some sort of stream or river nearby. You feel compelled to go toward the sounds, and before you think about it, you are on your feet. You open your eyes, which have been closed all along, and then you realize that you can see the wildlife that you had been blinded to when you had first entered the great jungle. You have grown accustomed to the sights around you, and you find that it is much easier to spot everything around you, and suddenly, you can see all of the beautiful, colorful birds that surround you. You can see them all, hiding in the trees.

Listening closely, you think that you can follow the sound of the river as it flows past the rock. You follow it, feeling compelled to discover where it is, and you head off to locate it. You are looking everywhere that you can for the source of the sounds, and you think that you have found it. Each step moves with more and more purpose as you go toward the sound, and soon, you see it.

There is a small stream of water, babbling over smooth stones in every shade of grey that you can imagine. There is not much water there; only perhaps a few inches and it would be easy to simply walk through it. On the other side of the stream, you can see that there is a pathway that seems to follow it, and you decide to cross. As you step into the water, you can feel it flow over your feet, cool and refreshing as it does. It laps around your toes as you walk carefully and with purpose across the stream. The rocks within it are smooth, but noticeably bumpy as you go over them, and soon, you are over the stream altogether.

The trail takes you on a winding path that follows the course of the stream, and the further you follow it, the more the stream seems to flow. As you walk, you can see it slowly swell up in power, and you realize that you must be getting closer to the water source. As you continue, you hear the sound off water becoming louder and louder, and soon, you are walking alongside what appears to be a cliff, with the ground on one side of you and the water on the other. You follow it around a bend, and you see it: A waterfall.

It is at least ten feet tall and the water cascaded over the ledge, creating a bubbling current right underneath it. The water appears white at the base, very quickly fading into the deep blue of the river that the stream had eventually become. You are not sure how far you have walked, but it was a very long way, and looking up at the sky, you realize that the sun is beginning to go down. It is time to make the long journey home.

CHAPTER 6: THE MOONLIT GARDEN

Imagine that you have just woken up. The sky is still dark, and upon glancing at your clock, you see that it is very late at night. Your entire home is sleeping and you cannot hear a single thing. The silence is almost deafening over you, and you slowly swing your legs over the side of the bed, pushing yourself up to standing. You decide that what you need is a quick walk so you can fall back asleep without any problems.

Your bedroom carpet is plush underneath your feet—it is squishy and soft, giving under each step that you take and dampening the sounds. Slowly and quietly, so as to not wake anyone else in your home, you make your way to the door to your home, compelled to keep walking by some unknown force or desire. You feel like you need to keep walking, so you do, quietly noticing the way that your body moves when you let it. It is loose, unencumbered by the stress or tension of the day. You feel perfectly relaxed as you move, and you know that you are going to exactly where you need to be.

You leave your home and quietly shut the door behind you. The nighttime is alive and abuzz with the sounds of everything else that, like you, is awake amidst the darkness. But, on that night, it is not particularly dark; the sky, and the world beneath it, is brightly illuminated by the biggest full moon that you have ever seen, made brighter by the faint haze of a wispy cloud that hangs over it at that moment in time. However, that cloud would not remain in place for very long, for the wind is gently blowing around you, and you can see that, just beyond the cloud is nothing but clear night sky.

In the distance, you can hear the buzzing sounds of crickets chirping around you. They sing their songs loudly and boldly, and you decide that, since you have nothing better to do on that late night, you will walk toward it. You follow the chirping of crickets, punctuated only by the occasional soft hoot of a bat, or the billowing of wind through the leaves. You walk through grass, which is cool and soft beneath your feet, and tickles between your toes a little bit as you go. You pass through the yard to an area that is lined with trees, and you keep going past them. You keep on moving, and soon, you approach what appears to be a garden. The garden is in a vast clearing that is lined by a wave of trees that appeared to have been grown there intentionally. The trees are lined up, creating a wall against the nighttime sky, but above you, you can still see the moon hanging in the air. The moon is no longer obscured, you quietly note to yourself, and the cloud seems to have disappeared completely. Instead, you see what looks like thousands of stars all overhead. You can see what appears to be a purplish streak, almost cloudy in appearance, throughout the sky, and you know that it is the Milky Way galaxy.

You stop and marvel at the sky for a moment. It is rare that you get a moment to truly disconnect, stop, and look at the sky, but in that moment, you have that. You have nothing pressing to be dealing with and you have no reason not to try to enjoy the stillness of the night around you, reveling in its quiet calmness in a way that you cannot do amidst the hustle and bustle of daily life.

Before long, you hear a sound behind you; a quiet rustling in the flowers that grow across the ground, and you turn to look at them. There is nothing there but the wind, but with it came the soft, sweet scent of roses and the other flowers perfuming the air around you. You walk toward the flowers, kneeling down when you get to them.

The first plant that you see is a beautiful rosebush. You can see that the buds are beginning to open up, and there are a few flowers that appeared to have already opened up entirely. The soft, silky petals are the color of the sunset. They are orange-ish in the center, and they fade into a soft, satiny pink color at the tips, beautifully and warmly. Just like the sunset, they bring to you feelings of comfort and peace, as well as a feeling of finality. They are soothing and welcoming, and you begin to feel a bit sleepy as you run your fingers across the delicate petals of the rose.

You look over, and you can see that the garden is filled with endless different flowers, ranging greatly from type to type. There are some flowers that are light pink and growing in bunches, straight up from the stems. There are some that are purple and delicate, swinging in the breeze. Others are red and others still are yellow. You look around the garden, and you can see that each and every flower is a different color. You can see that they all come together, carefully planted at just the right distance apart from each other so they can all grow, and there is not a weed in sight. The entire garden must be well maintained, you tell yourself as you look around.

You settle down to look at the flowers around you, enjoying the gentle garden that you are surrounded by, and then you see something. As another warm, gentle breeze blows past you, you see something light up, and then another something and another something after that. There are fireflies gently rising up and out of the garden into the sky above it. They flash their beautiful colors, each of them existing in a different color altogether. Some are brighter and others are dulled considerably. There are yellows that flicker and shine like incandescent streetlights that move about, up and down, and side to side. There are greens that appear to be bright green, the color of neon lights. Others still look red and pink. They are all vastly different colors, and they all dance in the air above the flowers.

You sit and watch their intricate dances as they buzz about each other, the lights seeming to almost pulse as they float on the gentle breeze. The sounds of their buzzing is gentle in the air and it harmonizes with the chirps of the crickets and the drone of the katydids in the distance. You enjoy their private show, reveling in the secrecy of it all and enjoying the gentle swaying of the insects as they go.

Occasionally, you see a moth drift through the fireflies, and the fireflies all clear the way, creating a wave of darkness as the moth drifts past, but beyond that, not a single animal comes to visit as you watch the show, until you notice something else: You hear the sound of a gentle hoot behind you.

Turning around, you see an owl staring at you. It is perched atop a low-hanging branch near you. The owl has a warm, brownish plumage, mottled in colors of yellowish, cream, and darker brown. Its head is smooth and it has a white, heart-shaped face with two big, brown eyes that stare closely at you. The owl's beak appears small, almost tucked away, and all you can see, shining in the moonlight, is its face. It tilts its head as you meet its gentle gaze and you can see that it seems to be considering what you want. It is curious about you, almost lazily so as it watches you, as if silently telling you to get a move on with it already.

Before you can do a thing, however, the owl suddenly spreads its wings to reveal the massive wingspan that it has, and it crouches down. You can see the power in its body as it pushes off from the branch, hard enough to make it dip down and wave helplessly in the air as an impressive stroke of wings lifts the owl into the air. It flaps its wings harder and harder, and yet, you do not hear a single sound—the flapping sound that you are accustomed to hearing in the daytime when a bird passes by is entirely silent as the owl goes overhead, treating you to the sight of its white body, speckled lightly with greys and creams on the chest as it flies away.

You are left, in awe, of the sight that you have seen, but you are also beginning to feel incredibly sleepy as well. All of that energy that you had from when you had woken up seems to have left you, and suddenly, you feel that intense urge to sleep fall over you. You are ready to sink back into your bed, so off you go after one last glance at the fireflies in their dance. You allow the memory of the fireflies to seal itself in your memory and off you go, retracing the steps that you took. Occasionally, you notice the owl flying overhead, as if it is guarding over you as you return home. It goes from tree to tree, flying out of sight, but always returning back to you.

When you arrive back at your door, you look over your shoulder one last time. Perched on the railing to your porch, you see the owl. It is looking at you, black eyes gleaming in the light from your porch and it tilts its head. You get the feeling that it is laughing at you, or at least, it would be if owls could laugh, and you feel yourself smile as you turn the cool doorknob in your hand. You debate saying something, but you are not sure that you knew what you were looking at, and you were even less sure that you knew that the owl was even able to understand you. Instead, you settle for a slight dip of your head in acknowledgement to the owl, and you find yourself pleasantly surprised when it nods its head right back to you in return. Was it coincidence or intentional? You may never know, but that's okay.

You make your way upstairs and into your bed, pleased to notice that no one else had woken up during your midnight romp through the garden, and you slip into bed. The mattress feels more inviting than it ever was before as you find just the right spot for you. You feel your body melting into the bed, releasing all of the tensions that you did not realize that you had, and you relax. With a deep breath in and out, you feel yourself calming down. You feel warm and comforted, more than ever before. You feel the waves of tiredness coming over you, little by little, and quietly, in the comfort of your bed, you drift right back to sleep.

CHAPTER 7: ADVENTURES IN THE SKY

Imagine for a moment that you are standing on the edge of a cliff that overlooks what appears to be the whole world. You can see for miles and miles in all directions as you stand atop the cliff, and in the distance, you can even see the ocean, dark blue and shimmering in the daylight. You do not feel afraid at all as you stand there, feet on the edge of what may have been the biggest plummet in the entire world. You are not afraid of falling because falling is exactly what you intend to do.

Strapped to you, you have a hang glider. Though you cannot turn around to see it, you know that the one that you have picked out is a cerulean blue, with a creamy white chevron across it. You have been training for this day for weeks, and you are finally ready to take to the sky for the very first time. You have the utmost trust that you will be able to fly and land safely, and you are ready to go.

Next to you, the coach that trained you checks on all of your harnesses one last time, tugging and tightening them to make sure that they are just right. Everything seems to be right and ready to go, as you get the thumbs up from the coach, who waves you off.

You take a big, deep breath and you steel yourself for the impossibility of what you are about to do. While you are unafraid, your body seems to resist the idea of jumping into oblivion with nothing more than a lightweight frame covered with cloth to protect you. You can feel the adrenaline flowing through your body. You can feel the protest in your legs, but you refuse to let it hold you back. Instead, you take a running leap into the air. You run as quickly as you can and throw yourself off of the ledge.

Immediately, as soon as the ground is no longer underneath your feet, you feel your breath hitch in your chest, and just as quickly, the wind fills the sails of your hang glider. You pull back and up suddenly, but you know exactly what to do. You position yourself just right, and you hang horizontally over the ground. You feel completely exposed as you hang in the air, at the complete mercy of the wind currents that keep you afloat. You are in the air for as long as the air allows. You are able to go where the wind takes you, with some direction that you can provide. You are there and in the moment.

You look ahead of yourself for a moment, and you see that, for as far as you can see, there is nothing but the sky. You see the clear, deep blue sky for miles and miles. There are occasionally birds that fly past you, almost surprised to see a human hanging out in your domain, but they do not protest; they simply let you pass them by without a single word. They fly quickly beyond you, leaving you to your solitude. You do not mind this at all, and as the wind gently guides you around the world, you are thrilled to explore the world. You can feel a wide grin on your face as you slowly direct your gaze downward to see the world underneath you.

The world is green underneath you and the trees look like heads of broccoli from your height. They are bumpy and green, but beyond the round circles of their crowns, you cannot make out the branches or leaves from your position. The bumps in the earth, making up the terrain that you know to be bumpy, looks like paper that had gotten water spilled upon it and then was left out to dry—it is wavy and shadowed in some areas, and you are surprised to see the strange texture. Despite your surprise, you feel ecstatic to be so incredibly high above the ground. You can see that there is a city in the distance, far from you. It looks like an ant colony from so far away. You are thrilled to see the sights and you realize just how expansive civilization is. You can see just how far the city seems to stretch out around you, and you see the roads weaving all around the terrain, appearing to be little more than lines on a map from so high up.

In the distance, you can see the beautiful water shimmering, and you can see the tiny white dots of what you assume are ships nearby. They are barely more than blips on the wide, open sea, and yet there is something about them that is beautiful as they slowly and lazily make their way across the water's surface. You are so high up that you cannot see the waves in the ocean from that distance, but you know that there are probably surfers going by. You know that there are people probably all over the beach at the moment, enjoying the beautiful, warm weather, just like you are in that moment.

You turn the hang glider toward an open field. You can feel that you are starting to lose altitude a bit and you know that your trip will not last forever. You know that you must aim to land on the open field to avoid running into any buildings or trees, and off you go.

As you continue to fly through the air, you realize that there is a flock of birds underneath you—they are geese that are honking at each other as they make their way through the air. They do not seem to realize that you are there, you realize as you look down at them. It is not every day that you are above a flock of geese and you take the moment to watch them as they move. They are surprisingly graceful as they move by, flapping their wings with powerful strokes of air. You smile as you watch them, feeling captivated by the strength that their wings had to have been feeling. You watch as they fly away and eventually veer off in another direction, making their way toward what you assume is the pond that you can see off to your right. They have much more control over where they are going than you do, you note, but that is okay; you are still enjoying your trip.

You feel a gust of wind, and suddenly, your hang glider gets pulled upwards. Your stomach feels like it jolts at the sudden change of altitude, and you grin. It looks like your journey isn't over yet after all! You get pulled up back to the height that you had started, and you begin to drift in the air, soaring further and faster now than you were before. You suddenly become aware of how cold your hands feel as they are whipped by the wind in the air around you. You are not surprised at all by the sensation, and so you wiggle your fingers a little bit against the metal in hopes of warming them up.

You are above what appears to be a small farm now. You can see how the ground looks like patchwork underneath you, with different colors on each. They appear stripy from your position in the sky, and the farmhouse that you can see near it looks so small that it could be a child's block or another toy. The farm rolls gently over the hills, and you are pretty sure that the tiny black dots that you see underneath you across a big, green pasture, are horses or cows wandering around, grazing on the food that they can get while they can get it.

You turn your glider again, trying to once again redirect it back toward the field that you planned on going to. You know that there will be people waiting there to pick you up in a little truck; they were there to pick you and your coach up the last time you went gliding with him while you were learning. You fly toward the open field and take one last moment to really relish in the weightlessness of what you are doing. You are thrilled at this experience that you got to enjoy and it is an almost indescribable feeling of joy within your chest as you fly through the air with little more than a plastic bar to keep you afloat.

As you continue off, you know that you have to begin to slow down the glider. As much as you would have preferred to keep flying at that current pace, you push down on the bar. You force yourself to slow down, just as you were taught when you were being trained. You push down on the bar as hard as you could, feeling the hang glider catch in the air as it begins to drag on the wind. You notice that you start to veer off to the left and you shift over to the right with your weight to get back on course.

You begin your descent, slowly and surely flying down closer and closer to the earth. You can feel the air begin to slow down as you get closer to the ground, and you watch as the trees, which looked like toys at first, grow bigger and bigger as you approach them. You watch with a mixture of awe and disappointment as the sky gets further and further and as you return back to the ground beneath your feet.

As you get close enough to the ground to land, you push back on the bar as hard as you can. You know that you have to tilt the nose of the glider up and over to make the glider sort of stall out, and you make it happen. The glider stops flying through the sky and begins to fall, but you are close enough to the ground that you can plant your feet, stopping the glider in its tracks.

Somehow, you do it, and you find that you are standing there, disheveled, on solid ground, and suddenly feeling like you are moving significantly slower than you were before, and you are—you are no longer moving at all. You feel the firmness of the ground under your feet, steady and in control, and you are thrilled to have enjoyed it.

CHAPTER 8: THE SUNSET

Take in a deep breath and close your eyes. As you do, imagine that you are sitting in a vast meadow. It is a meadow filled with beautiful grass that seems to roll on endlessly around you, whispering as the wind gently carries it. You are atop a picnic blanket that you have brought with you; the blanket itself is soft, quilted of cotton, and gently patted. It is your favorite color, given to you by a dear friend. You have plenty of good memories of this blanket and you are glad to have it with you at that point in time. You sigh and take in a big, deep breath to yourself and allow yourself to relax. You are more comfortable than you have been in a very long time.

The meadow smells softly of warm grass and of buttercup flowers that seem to grow all around you in little patches, scattered throughout the grass. They spatter the endless green with bright patches of yellow, almost like butterflies as they wave in the gentle breeze. The world is very quiet around you aside from the whispers of the wind, and you bask in the comfort and the relaxation that you draw from it.

On the horizon, you notice that the sky is beginning to change. The sun is beginning to grow heavy, dropping lower than ever on the horizon. As it does, it shifts from bright white to a hazy orange. The once-blue sky is becoming tinged with the splash of oranges and reds as the sun gets closer and closer to the mountains that you can see cutting the horizon, carving out the space between the land and the sky. The sun is hovering just above one of the mountain peaks, and the sky is ablaze with beautiful watercolor colors. Pinks and purples spill across the sky, washing over the blue. They dance through the clouds, reflecting more light and painting the sky further with streaks of blueish grey, illuminated with pinks on the underside as the sun drops beneath them on the horizon line.

Far off behind you, as if chasing after the sun, you can see the dusky blue streaks of nighttime beginning to reach out. The sky is darkening into nighttime, and you know that it will not be long, at this rate, that the sun will disappear, leaving behind nothing but the navy blue blanket of nighttime. Yet, despite knowing that it is getting later, you make no attempt to move away.

You watch as the fiery oranges of sunset begin to give way to pinks as the first part of the sun dips beyond the mountains. You watch as the pinks bathe the entire land in sunset colors, and you watch as the sun finally dips beyond the horizon, leaving behind the purples of twilight. The clouds closest to the horizon still seem to glow orange with the sun's light, and the sky begins to turn into a dusky lavender color, blending into the navy blue on the horizon.

All around you, the wildlife seems to shift. What was once quiet, aside from the occasional buzz of a bumblebee blundering its way through the world became the chirps of crickets all around you. You can see the first star—the Morning Star that you know better by the name of Venus in the night sky. It shimmers in the purple with a steady light, brighter than anything else in the nighttime sky aside from the moon. You can see it there, just beyond the horizon and over the mountains. It gleams there, and you watch it for a while, marveling at the distance between yourself and the planet. It is so wondrous that you can see an entirely different planet that exists so far away!

The chirps of crickets is soon joined by the drones of katydids and you sigh to yourself, leaning backwards onto the blanket. This is what you were really here for—the nighttime sky. You watch above you as the navy blue blanket of nighttime begins to wash out the purple, slowly and steadily creeping across the sky, little by little. You can watch as the darkness seems to grow further and further across the sky and you feel calm as you watch it.

Soon, you see another star appear in the sky. It suddenly appears, a tiny pinprick of white light on the darkness of night. And then, another appears, twinkling away not too far from the first one. You watch as little by little, stars continue to appear in front of you. You watch as they make their way throughout the sky, gleaming brightly. You are thrilled to watch and as each one appears in the sky, you feel even more at ease. You feel more relaxed into the blanket underneath you.

A cool breeze drifts through the area, and you realize for the first time, that the air has a slight nighttime chill to it. It is not too cold, but it is noticeably cooler than the warmth of daytime. You pull on your jacket that you had brought with you and you slide it on, eager to keep away any mosquitoes or other bugs that may buzz their way over to you. Immediately, the jacket wraps around you and warms you up just enough for you to continue watching on.

You look up at the sky and you see a tiny dot blinking with light as it passes over you. It is far away, further than any airplane that you have ever seen, and shining brightly. It lazily makes its way across the night sky as you watch it with mild interest. It must be a satellite, you tell yourself, watching the way it slowly makes its way across the sky and away from your sight. You eventually lose track of it and go right back to stargazing. It is the perfect night to be exploring space all around you and there is not a single cloud in the sky. You watch as the moon slowly becomes visible, peeking out over the horizon as well and moving its way across the sky. It is a crescent moon—barely there—and that makes the sky that much darker for the nighttime viewing that you have decided to take.

As you watch, you see a few airplanes pass by, so far away that you cannot hear them, but their blinking lights are unmistakable as they come, and then they go, and you are once again left in the solitude of the night sky around you. The sky is filled up with stars by this point, with them appearing everywhere that you can see.

You smile to yourself, thankful that you are so far away from the city that the sky is incredibly dark and you are shocked at just how many stars that you can see all around you. You knew that space was full of stars and that they were everywhere throughout the universe, but you never realized just how many of them that you did not usually see in the sky around you. You did not realize just how beautiful the sky can be, and you revel in the inky blackness that has gently fallen over the night sky. You look at the stars, watching as they all twinkle in their own dances, to their own rhythms, and with their own colors as they dance in place to their own tunes.

As you are watching, lost in your own thoughts as you look at the sky, movement in the corner of your eye catches your attention. You turn your focus to see what you noticed, and just then, you see a shooting star. It comes and goes in a white streak across the black sheet of night, slicing through the darkness with its own gentle glow, glimmering in place for a split second before it fizzled out, leaving nothing but the night sky behind. However, you stopped and waited for a moment, waiting to see if anything else would appear, and sure enough, a second shooting star shot across, as if it were chasing after the one that had vanished the first time.

The two shooting stars had both faded away just as quickly as they had appeared, and you feel a mix of feelings in response. You are happy that you got to see them and marvel at yet another of the universe's greatest mysteries, and yet you were also somewhat disappointed that it had vanished so quickly as well. They were gorgeous in the moment, and yet, you had nothing left of them but that memory that they had burned into your mind.

Instead of dwelling, you turn your attention right back to the stars in the sky, watching them twinkle just a little bit longer. You slow down your breathing as you do, breathing in slowly as you look from star to star across the endless stars throughout the entire sky. You are in awe of the celestial beauty, and you feel comfort knowing that you can come back to this scene any time that you want; you know that it is deep within your heart and your mind, and you can go back to explore it any time that you want to.

You realize something—the moon has traveled quite far on its journey. It has made its way from the horizon to right above you, and you realize that you are unsure how much time has passed. You decide that it has gotten late enough and you pack up all of your belongings to head back home, knowing that you will be back to visit this beautiful meadow again sometime.

CHAPTER 9: THE BLAZING MOUNTAIN

Imagine for a moment that you have just opened your eyes to find yourself amidst a beautiful grove. You can feel cool, crisp mountain air all around you, and a glance at your surroundings tells you that you are, in fact, standing about halfway up a mountain with crystal clear skies above you. You look around you and you realize that the trees that are in front of you have long, thin white trunks. The trunks are covered in black spots, almost like hundreds of eyes, all on you as you look around at all of the trees. You study them closely, slowly bringing your gaze from their trunks and up to their foliage. They are covered in shockingly yellow leaves, as if someone had taken the dust of buttercups and goldenrods and plastered them atop the leaves. They are aspen trees, standing tall and proud in a grove amidst the great pine trees that stretch out toward the heavens, reaching upwards with their evergreen needles.

You take in a deep breath and you recognize the smell of autumn hanging in the air. It smells of pine and soil, but also of that sweet scent of leaves that are turning yellow, earthy and primal, and yet pleasantly enjoyable. You feel at ease in the smell of sweetness that engulfs the air, accentuated by the sharp scent of pine that lingers around you. It is the scent of change; of the world moving forward and preparing to sleep. It is the scent of an end that will bring with it a new beginning, and it is incredibly soothing.

As you breathe in the air, feeling it stretch out your lungs and fill them up again with ease, you realize just how crisp the chilly air is. You are well-protected—you are wearing a jacket and boots, and you are not cold at all, but the air has that nearly winter chill to it and you cannot help but grin as you feel it. You take a step forward and feel the leaves give way under your boots. When you look down for the first time, you realize that the ground is painted yellow and red with all of the leaves that have already descended from the trees to blanket the ground, and with each step that you take, you kick up more and more leaves, adding more of the sweet scent to the air as you do so.

Somewhere in the distance, you hear a crow cawing out, but no matter how much you look around, you cannot see it. As you listen to the papery sounds of the leaves rubbing together, you also hear something else—the sound of water lapping against rocks. You follow the sound, seeing trees that look straight out of a paint palette with how brightly colored they are. The grasses are all turning golden and the leaves in the trees are every shade between yellow and red imaginable, brightening up the scenery one last time before winter will completely and totally take over everything around you. You keep moving forward, and soon, you find a small creek cascading down the mountain. It babbles as it goes over the rocks and you sit for a while to listen. You do not think that you will be spending too much time there, but you do know one thing is for sure: the picture of the creek as it slowly trickles down the mountain, surrounded by the trees the color of a blazing fire is beautiful.

You take your leave after a while, eventually finding a trail, from what it looks like. You can see old boot prints in the ground, imprinting where there used to be people walking around, but most of the trail appears to be completely coated in freshly fallen leaves. You can just barely make out the dirt on the ground as you continue on your way.

The trail eventually curves around and you decide to follow it for a while, continuing up higher and higher to see where it leads. You can hear birds tweeting every now and then, and the occasional buzzing of insects as your feet crunch through the leaves to your pace. You enjoy the path as you continue to walk, enjoying the solitude that it brings. You may not know how high up you are, but you do know one thing; it is so beautiful, you do not care.

Eventually, as you continue to walk, you hear the chattering of a squirrel nearby. The squirrel is interested in you, watching you from atop a leafless branch. It is holding onto an acorn, watching you closely for a moment. You watch it, too. It twitches its bushy rust-colored tail and scampers away, up the tree trunk and out of sight.

You continue on your way after the squirrel takes its leave, wandering around to see what else you can find. Soon, the trees start to become scarcer. They stop creating a dense forest as you get higher and higher up the mountain. You look down on the ground and realize that it has become much rockier. You must be approaching the tree line, you tell yourself, and you keep moving up. And soon, there appear to be no plants left at all; you are surrounded entirely by rocks atop the peak of the mountain. As you break free from the trees, you are able to look out around you, and then the sudden gravity of how high up you are hit. You feel weak in the knees as you look out above yourself. You look around in awe; you can see for miles. The cities off in the distance look like tiny blips on the horizon, and you can see roads leading to the mountains like tiny snakes beneath you, little more than minute trails scattered across the landscape.

All around you, you can see more mountains coming up, and the breath in your chest catches; you realize that they are all ablaze with the same bright colors of autumn that you had been studying earlier. You can see the same colors shooting all across the environment, painting the mountains beautiful warm golds, browns, reds, with the occasional green of some pine trees intermixed. It looks as if someone had spilled paints all over what was normally a green, or even white with winter, landscape.

You sit down on the rocks beneath you. The coldness of the stone can be felt through your pants as you sit and you marvel at the wonders of the world that you have just conquered. You are sitting atop one of the highest vantage points that you can be on—you are above all of the towers and above all of the buildings that exist in a city. You are higher than most people on the ground underneath you. You are able to see for miles and miles, until the sky and the earth collide on the horizon, and for the first time in a while, just how small you, as a person, are weighs heavily on you. You feel in awe of just how high up the mountain that you are and you are thrilled to be given that gift.

As you sit atop the world, contemplating just how high up you are, you see something—an eagle. It is flying past you, but seems to notice that you are there. It lands near where you are sitting and it stares at you. You can see its big, golden eye looking right back at you and you watch it, unsure what to do next. Then, the eagle moves over a bit higher up from where you are and it lands atop another rock. You look up at it and are surprised to see something hidden amongst the rocks. It is an eagle's nest and the eagle is sitting in the nest, watching you warily.

Soon, another eagle flies by, and just like the first one, it sits atop the same rock and watches you closely. It is highly interested in what you are doing, and it makes no move to join its mate. Instead, it lowers its head, its hooked beak dipping down toward the ground, and it watches you closely.

When you watch the eagle, you realize something; it seems to be entirely unafraid of you. It seems unfazed by the fact that it is sitting right next to you as it stares at you proudly. You can't help but feel a little bit intimidated about it and its large, sharp claws that are currently gripping the rock tightly as it does stare you down.

You hold your breath and you wait to see what it will do.

You and the eagle stare at each other closely for a long while, and then you see it shift. You see it tense its muscles in its legs, and you watch as it launches itself into the sky as quickly as it can muster. It throws itself forward, wings pounding to fight off gravity, and it wins with ease. You marvel at its grace as it dances through the air, flying higher.

Then, the other eagle joins it; they both fly up high into the air before they lock talons together, and at first, you think that they are going to fight. Then, you realize something, they seem to be working together. They spiral through the air together, holding each other's talons as they both spin toward the round, dancing together. They disappear beyond the trees and you can no longer see them.

You stop for a moment, wondering what to do. They seemed to be perfectly fine. You hold your breath, and then, just as suddenly as they had disappeared, you see both birds flying high above you again as they return back to their nest, together. They had done it intentionally together, and you decide that you have intruded on their time enough. You make your way right back down the mountain, retracing your steps back the best that you could.

CONCLUSION

And with that, you have arrived to the end of *Bedtime Stories for Adults*. Hopefully, this book has brought with it many sleep-filled nights that have been able to guide you through getting the rest that you crave, and the rest that you need. Sleep, as necessary as it is, is also incredibly fickle. It is incredibly easy to disrupt sleep in endless fashions, from anxiety and intrusive thoughts to problems with the lifestyle that you are living and about a million in-between possibilities.

CPSIA information can be obtained
at www.ICGtesting.com
Printed in the USA
LVHW021114260521
688447LV00012B/669